Facilitator's Guide

for use with

Mystie's Activities for Bereaved Children Grades K - 2

and

For the Love of Emrys

KIDS' GRIEF RELIEF

Hi, I'm Mystie.
What's
Dragon - You - Down ?

www.KidsGriefRelief.org

A 501(c)(3) NonProfit

Grief Support to Empower Bereaved Children

ISBN: 978-0-9856334-6-2
(softcover book)

Congratulations on deciding to facilitate a student bereavement group!

Your great contribution is giving your students the opportunity to process their grief over the death of a loved one, while empowering them with life affirming skills. This program is not a substitute for professional counseling. It is a program to support students to move through their grief themselves as you create a safe and loving environment.

Validation of their challenging experience, no matter how extreme, is crucial. It creates a foundation of unconditional love and acceptance, which is the perfect environment for the success of this course. The validating conversation helps your students understand that their reactions to the death are normal. It helps them see that no matter how "dire" the situation may look, they have the ability to not only move through their grief, but be stronger for their experience. As you practice empathy instead of sympathy, you place yourself in a position to support your student's journey through grief.

The activities in this program are geared for younger children. It's possible that the same children will need a program again, as they mature.

Grief is not an experience students "get over". It's an experience they move through. Ultimately, the death of a loved one becomes integrated into their lives. They can then use this experience to help them gain an awareness of their inner power to move through any of life's challenges.

Our deepest intention is that this course supports each student with the knowledge of the power of Changeless Love within them. Change is inevitable, as realized with the death of a loved one. Yet Love remains forever. It's ongoing expression creates a fulfilling life, moment by moment.

Blessings,
Kids' Grief Relief

Program Guidelines

- This is a grade-specific, *Activity-Based* program which consists of this Facilitator's Guide, and a Student's Booklet of 31 Activities (i.e. ***Mystie's Activities***) which students use to construct their own Activity Book.

- This a a Six-Session Program; ideally one Session per week (we recommend no more than two Sessions per week). The Six Sessions are titled:

  - **What is Grief ?**
  - **My Memories**
  - **My Story**
  - **I Can Help Myself**
  - **My Thoughts Matter**
  - **Ending Celebration**

- The Program is written for groups, and works best when students can interact with each other. It can easily and effectively be used for one child, by selecting activities that do not involve other's participation. We recommend that no more than six students be in a group.

- Each Session contains multiple activities about the specified theme. There are enough activities to last about 45 minutes to one hour per session. The number of activities accomplished is a function of the number of students, the allotted time, the amount of discussion, and the choice to either do the activities verbally or in written form.

- It is recommended that the students receive a folder to store their *Mystie's Activities* book/ pages, and personal photos of their loved one.

- For each Session, the facilitator directs the students to the chosen Activities. Some Activites are only generated by the facilitator, so there is no cooresponding numbered activity in the booklet (e.g. Activity 17 - What Would Mystie Say?).

Program Guidelines

- *Mystie's Activities* are referenced by activity number (e.g. Activity 8). The Activity number is located at the lower corner of each page (e.g. Activity 9A). These 31 activities are designed to be a written record of each student's experience. For students who are unable to write, we recommend someone write their responses for them.

- If it's not possible to get all the written activities completed in one session, activities can be done orally, keeping the goal of the session in focus. For example, in Activity 12 (*Things To Remind Me*), if there isn't enough time for students to write their list, they can orally share their favorite mementos and tell the class where they keep them.

- Collect the folders at the end of each session. The culmination of all the activity sheets becomes each student's personal Activity Book, a keepsake awarded at the end of the program. It is a written record of their participation and achievement.

- For each activity, read over the complete procedure before you present it. You know your students best. You may want to skip some steps or add something of your own. Skip any activity that does not fit your student's needs.

- Some children may express a desire to cut, staple or tape specific Activities. If time permits, and resources are available, we suggest you support the child's request.

- Encourage students to bring to class pictures and memorabilia of their loved ones. Always allow time for students to share these items. Note the terms "special person" and "loved one" are used interchangeably in reference to the one for whom the student is grieving.

- If you have any questions regarding this program, please email us at inquiry@kidsgriefrelief.com

Required Facilitator Materials

For All Six Sessions:

Markers/crayons/pens/pencils

Mystie's Activities for Bereaved Children Grades 3 - 5

Facilitator's Guide

Mystie Mobile

Folder for each student

Additional Needed Materials:

Session#1

Session#2

Game Markers and One Die

Candy for prizes

Sessions#3 and #4

For the Love of Emrys

Mystie Mobile

Session#5

Waste Basket

Scrap paper

Hand mirror

Session#6

Battery operated tea-lights for each student

Food & Drinks for students

*Optional: Graduation Gift for each student ***

*Kids' Grief Relief sells special **Mystie** gifts for children who have completed the course. Go to www.kidsgriefrelief.org/Products.html to choose and order the most appropriate items for each student.*

CLASS SYLLABUS

Class Syllabus

Session #1
<u>What Is Grief?</u>

1. Introduction
2. Getting Acquainted
3. What Is Grief ?
4. What Am I Feeling ?

5. Expressing My Feelings
6. How Does My Body Feel ?
7. Circle of Trust

Session #2
<u>My Memories</u>

8. I Practice Compassion
9. My Support Group
10. My Favorite Memory

11. Roll-A-Memory Game
12. Things to Remind Me

Session #3
<u>My Story</u>

13. Am I Still Dragged-Down ?
14. Reading <u>For the Love of Emrys</u>

15. Dramatizing the Story
16. My Story

Class Syllabus

Session #4
I Can Help Myself

Session #5
My Thoughts Matter

Session #6
Ending Celebration

Session 1
What is Grief ?

Objectives

- Children become comfortable talking about the death of their loved one.

- Children understand the many feelings associated with grief.

- Children accept their own feelings of grief.

- Children promise to keep confidentiality within the group.

Before handing out *Mystie's Activities* :

–Discuss why students are participating in a grief group.

–Discuss the importance of coming to each session.

–Discuss the level of participation: it's their own choice and it's okay not to share.

–Discuss using common courtesies, such as being quiet when someone is speaking, and showing respect to other members.

Session 1
What is Grief ?
Activities 1-7

Mystie's Activities

1A-B. Introduction

2. Getting Aquainted

3A-B. What Is Grief ?

4. What Am I Feeling ?

5. Expressing My Feelings

6. How Does My Body Feel ?

7. Circle of Trust

Activity 1 A-B
Introduction

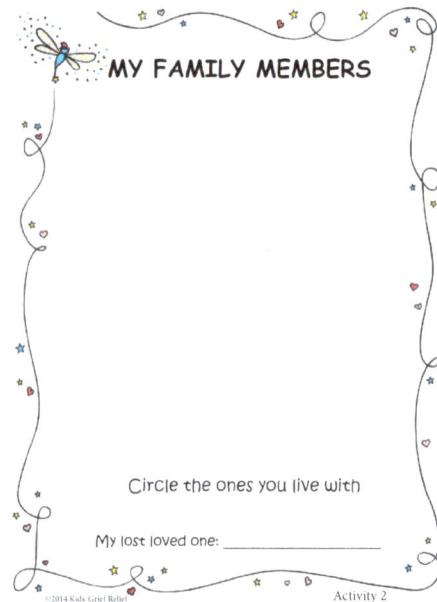

My Special Activity Booklet about _____ and me.

A-1   ©2011 Kids' Grief Relief

MY FAMILY MEMBERS

Circle the ones you live with

My lost loved one: _____

©2014 Kids' Grief Relief   Activity 2

Procedure:

- Direct children to fill in the blank at the top of the Activity 1A page.

- Direct them to draw a picture of their loved one with themselves.

- Direct students to fill out Activity 1B. Have them include Aunts/Uncles, Grandparents, and Pets.

Activity 2
Getting Aquainted

> Hi Kids!
> My name is Mystie. I'm a mystical, magical dragonfly from a far away planet.

> TIME TO SHARE

> What's your name?
>
> What grade are you in?
>
> How old are you?
>
> Who died?
>
> Share your cover picture with your group.

> ©2013 Kids' GriefRelief

Procedure:

- Read top of Activity 2.

- Go over each question on the page, giving children time to write down their answers, and/or speak their answers aloud.

- When children have completed this activity, ask them to share their front cover with the rest of the class.

Activity 3
What is Grief?

Are you feeling dragged—down because someone you love has died?

I felt dragged—down when my best friend suddenly died. I knew I would never see him again. It felt awful. I couldn't even fly.

I was feeling
GRIEF.

When I first flew to Earth, I thought Earth dragonflies lived forever like the dragonflies where I come from.

So when I met Darvy, the Earth dragonfly, I thought we would be friends for a long time. But I was wrong. Earth dragonflies have a short life.

Darvy and I had so much fun together! We flew wildly all over the marsh at the edge of the beach, where we lived. We laughed and played all day long. I loved being with him!

Then one day while we were playing dragonfly tag, he died. He suddenly stopped flying and fell to the ground. I was shocked. I felt terrible. I couldn't believe what happened.

We had a funeral, and buried him near a special rock where we used to sit and talk. I cried and cried.

I had a lot of different feelings. Some of the feelings are listed on the next page. What are YOU feeling?

Procedure:

- Read Activity 3A. Direct children to circle the word "GRIEF", telling them that grief is something we all feel when someone we love dies.

- Invite children to walk around the room looking "dragged-down" like Mystie. (head down and arms hanging down toward the floor)

- Say, "Let's read Mystie's story on the next page to find out why she felt so dragged-down."

- Read aloud Activity 3B. Ask children why Mystie felt dragged-down.

Activity 4
What Am I Feeling?

How are you feeling?
What are you thinking about? Do you know why you feel this way?
What do you wish would happen?

Good or Great
Positive or excellent ... no problems or worries!

OK
Acceptable but not great ... something seems out of place.

Friendly
Wanting to spend time with others or getting to know new people.

Loving
Wanting to hug or share because of a special connection or friendship.

Energetic
Lots of activity and physical expression coming from inside you that must come out!

Hopeful
Wishing for ... looking forward to ... or expecting something.

Stressed
Upset by what is happening and uncertain about the future.

Mad
Upset about something ... things are not going the way you want them to.

Confused
Can't think clearly, and not sure what's happening.

Lonely
Needing a friend or a hug ... being apart from others.

Sad
Not happy because something bad has happened to you or someone you know.

Shocked
Surprised, but not in a good way.

Feeling Something Else
You know how you feel, but it's not included on this chart.
Draw Your Emotion/Face Here

Feelings Keep Changing
You know how you feel, but it changes a lot. Or you're feeling a lot of different ways all at the same time.

What would you call this emotion/face?

This chart is color-ready. Just print and color!
Copyright © 2012 by Rainbow Fear (www.rainbowears.com).

3

Procedure:

- Show children the Mystie Mobile as you read Activity 4 with them.

- Go over all the listed feelings on Activity 4, directing children to circle the faces that describe the feelings of grief they are experiencing.

- Encourage children to add other feelings that are not listed, such as scared, frustrated, or upset.

- Listen for opportunities to suggest healthy ways to express their feelings, <u>emphasizing that it's not healthy to express feelings by hurting themselves or others</u>.

Activity 5
Expressing My Feelings

When I was feeling dragged—down about Darvy's death, the beautiful colors in my wings were all muddied up. I had so many feelings.

-----What colors show your feelings?-----

For example, what color shows you're sad?   ? Gray?

What color shows you're upset? You're worried?

Would   color in my wings   how you feel?

©2013 Kids' Grief Relief

Procedure:

- Read Activity 5 with children.

- Direct children to color Mystie's wings, then share why they chose their colors.

Activity 6
How Does My Body Feel?

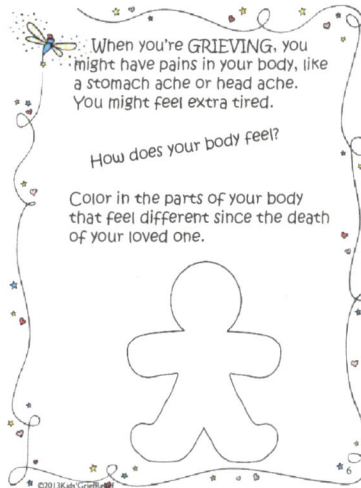

When you're GRIEVING, you might have pains in your body, like a stomach ache or head ache. You might feel extra tired.

How does your body feel?

Color in the parts of your body that feel different since the death of your loved one.

Procedure:

- Read Activity 6.

- As children color in parts of the drawing, ask them to explain what they are feeling.

- Tell students they will feel better as time passes, and as they continue to come to group and share about their feelings.

Activity 7
Circle of Trust

In the circle below, write down the names of all the children in your grief group, including yourself.

If you agree to keep confidential what is spoken in your group, trace over the circle.

Procedure:

- Read top of Activity 7 and direct children to fill in the circle with the appropriate names.

- Open a discussion about the importance of keeping what is said in grief group, confidential. Tell children it is not appropriate to share with children outside of class.

- Read the bottom of the Activity and direct children to outline the circle. This symbolizes their agreement not to speak about grief group outside of the group.

- End this initial session by congratulating the students for sharing about their grief. For the next session, ask children to bring in pictures or other printed materials (funeral program, obituaries) about their loved one.

"...There is an inate ability within all of us to move through life's challenging experiences with grace and strength. This includes the child..."

from *The Evolution of Child Bereavement*
by Kids' Grief Relief

Session 2
My Memories

Objectives

- Children recognize who is helping them with their grief.

- Children enjoy sharing special memories about their loved one.

- Children tell about their special momentos of their loved one.

Materials Needed:

Game markers & One Die

Candy for Prizes

Session 2
My Memories

Activities 8-12

Mystie's Activities

8. I Practice Compassion

9A-B. My Support Group

10. My Favorite Memory

11. Roll-A-Memory Game

12. Things To Remind Me

Activity 8
I Practice Compassion

Hi Kids! How are you feeling today?

Let's start today by practicing Compassion.
Compassion comes from a loving heart.
You can speak words of Compassion to other children in your group.
Having someone care helps a person who is feeling grief.

Here are some ideas of what to say.
As you listen and read the words, choose one to say to someone else in the group.

"Your _____ loved you a lot. I know you're going to miss her. I bet you have lots of great memories about her."

"I'm sorry to hear about the death of _____. You must miss him very much."

"I know you feel really sad about _____ dying. It's okay to feel sad and upset about it."

Procedure:

- Read Activity 8 with children.

- Ask children to repeat the phrases of Compassion, one at a time.

- Ask one child at a time to say one of the phrases to another student, so every child has the chance to say a phrase and to hear a phrase said to him/her.

22

Activity 9
My Support Group

Everyone grieves differently.

There's no right or wrong way.

You're grieving the way you need to.

It's okay to feel mad, sad or upset.

It's okay to cry.

I grieved for many months. Remember I told you how my beautiful wings were way dragged-down and muddied up when my friend died?

Eventually I felt better. My friend Lark, the dolphin, helped me alot. She listened to me and helped me understand that what I was feeling was normal.

Now I really LOVE to help children like you feel better!

In the heart below, write down the names of the people and pets who are helping you feel better.

Procedure:

- Read Activity 9A with children.

- Read top of Activity 9B, directing children to write their list of support people.

Activity 10
My Favorite Memory

Do you know what a memory is?

In the box below, draw a picture of your favorite memory with you loved one.

My Favorite Memory

Procedure:

• Read Activity 10.

• Children draw a picture of their favorite memory with their loved one.

• Children share their pictures with the rest of the group.

Activity 11
Roll-A-Memory Game

1 What is the first and last name of your special person ?	2 Did your special person teach you anything ?	3 Do you know your special person's birthday ? (Day/Month/Year)	4 Was your special person buried or cremated ?	5 Did your special person like to wear jewelery ? What kind ?
6 Describe a special holiday spent with your special person.	7 Tell about the last time you saw your special person.	8 What name did your special person call you ?	9 Tell about a funny moment with your special person.	10 Describe a trip you took with your special person.
11 Tell about what kind of clothes your special person liked to wear.	12 Tell about an object that reminds you of your special person.	13 What kind of music did your special person enjoy ?	14 What kind of movies did your special person like to watch ?	15 Did your special person ever have a pet ?
16 Did your special person have a favorite saying ? What was it ?	17 Tell about a sad memory with your special person.	18 Tell about some of the people who loved your special person.	19 What one thing always makes you think about your special person ?	20 What's your favorite photo of your special person ? Describe it.
21 Tell about something your special person loved to do.	22 What time of day do you feel "dragged-down" over the death of your special person ?	23 What's the one thing you'll miss MOST about your special person ?	24 Do you feel peaceful about the way your special person was buried ? Why ?	25 Tell about a gift you gave your special person.

©2014 Kids' Grief Relief   A-13

Procedure:
• This game requires game markers, a die and prizes. Each child has his/her own board, which is Activity 11.

Directions:
1. Each child chooses a marker.

2. Decide the order of players.

3. First child rolls the dice and moves that many spaces, left to right, along their board.

4. Read aloud the question on the square. If the child answers the question, direct him/her to draw a heart in the box.

5. If it is a question the child can not answer, direct him/her to put an X on the square and to skip over it the next time around. Direct the student to roll again until he/she lands on a question that can be answered, or on a prize space.

6. Play a few rounds until each child has at least 8 numbers circled.

Activity 12
Things To Remind Me

What special things do you have to remind yourself about your loved one who died? Make a list.

Where do you keep all your special things?

Procedure:

- Read Activity 12.

- As children list their mementos, ask them to share why each specific memento is important to them.

"...A 'healing space' is where the bereaved child is given the opportunity to speak to others without any judgement, receiving validation for his or her many feelings and thoughts associtiated with grief. As a dialogue opens up, the child begins the process of leading *themself* through healing"...

from *The Evolution of Child Bereavement*
by Kids' Grief Relief

Session 3
<u>My Story</u>

Objectives

- Children read *For the Love of Emrys* to explore how a young girl moves through grief.

- Children dramative this story to extend their understanding of grief.

- Children write and share their personal story of the death of their loved one.

<u>*Materials Needed:*</u>

For the Love of Emrys
Mystie Mobile

Session 3
My Story

Activities 13-16

Mystie's Activities

13. Am I Still Dragged-Down ?

14. Reading *For the Love of Emrys*

15. Dramatizing the Story

16A-B. My Story

Activity 13
Am I Still Dragged-Down?

Hi Kids! How are you feeling today?

Look at the mobile of me. Can you bend my wings to show everyone how you've been feeling the past week?

When you're grieving over someone, parts of you may be happy, yet parts may be still sad or upset.

Use my four wings to show your feelings.

14

Procedure:

• Read top of Activity 13 with children. Tell children they can either write some words or draw a picture to tell how they are feeling today.

• Read bottom of Activity 13. Give each child a chance to manipulate the wings of the Mystie mobile to show how he/she is feeling.

Activity 14
Reading *For the Love of Emrys*

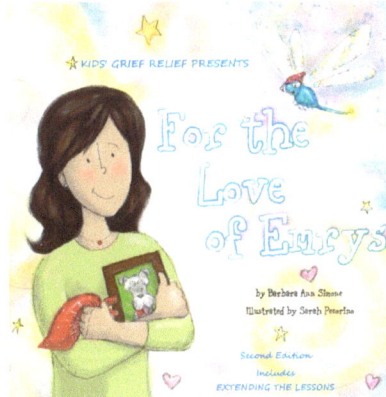

Procedure:

- As you read the title of the book, show cover to children and ask them what they think the story will be about.

- If they haven't guessed, tell children the story is about a little girl who is grieving over the death of her pet dog.

- Ask children if they think the story will be sad, and what Christina might do when her dog dies.

- Tell children that Mystie, the Magical dragonfly will help Christina feel better.

- Ask children what they think Mystie will do to help Christina.

- Read story to children, allowing for comments and questions on each page.

Activity 15
Dramatizing the Story

Procedure:

- Options to dramatize the story are listed on the next page.

- Choose as many as time permits.

Activity 15
Dramatizing the Story

Options to dramatize the story

- Ask one child to pretend to be Mystie, and another child to be Christina. Ask them to reennact the moment when Christina first meets Mystie, as Mystie says:

  "WHAT'S DRAGON-YOU-DOWN?"
  Allow children to continue their dialogue until Christina feels better. Depending on the number of children and time allotment, each child can pretend to be Mystie and Christina, one time.

- Use paper puppets to have children act out Mystie and Christina. They can be hand-drawn, or copied and cut out from the previous page ahead of time.

- Ask a child to be him/herself while another child pretends to be Mystie, saying,
  "WHAT'S DRAGON-YOU-DOWN?".
  Allow the child to tell Mystie what happened in his/her own life.

- A child can use the Mystie mobile in the play-acting of the story, while another child can pretend to be Christina.

Activity 16
My Story

Did you read about my friend Christina? I helped her when her dog died. She was really sad.

At the end of her story, Christina feels a lot better. She knows Emrys will always be in her heart. She has lots of love to share with others; she'll love them for the rest of her life.

A-16A

BEFORE Emrys died we played together every day. He listened to me and sat on my lap all the time. I loved to pet him and take care of him. My favorite time of the day was when we ran together. He was fast!

Tell about times BEFORE your loved one died.

I was with Emrys THE DAY HE DIED. He became very sick. His body stopped working. I took his body to the vet. I was upset and sad. It was hard to come home and see all his playthings. I wanted so much for him to be alive, but he wasn't.

Tell about THE DAY YOUR LOVED ONE DIED.

AFTER EMRYS DIED I felt very alone. No one will ever take his place in my heart. I think about him a lot. I am happy that we had so much fun when he was alive. As I grow up, I want to always remember how he loved me and how I loved him.

Tell about AFTER YOUR LOVED ONE DIED.

16

Procedure:

- Read Activity 16 A to children. Tell them it's their turn to share their story about what happaned when their loved one died.

- If children cannot write, we recommend that someone write their story for them.

- Read the story on the left side of Activity 16 B.

- Do the right side in the order it is printed. When all three sections are complete, invite each child to read his/her story from top to bottom.

"...Eventually, the grieving child is open to receive an understanding that all the thoughts and feelings of grief are a "normal" part of life. The child gives audience for a compassionate adult to support and lead him or her in finding their inner strength to heal. Understanding this lead role is a critical ingredient of the spiritual and emotional growth of the child"...

from *The Evolution of Child Bereavement*
by Kids' Grief Relief

Session 4
I Can Help Myself

Objectives

✦ Children share where they believe their loved one is.

✦ Children understand they can still show love for their deceased love one.

✦ Children learn ways to help themselves move through grief.

✦ Children learn how to do a *"belly-breath"* as a way to relax when they are upset.

Materials Needed:
Mystie Mobile
For the Love of Emrys

Session 4
I Can Help Myself

Activities 17-21

Mystie's Activities

17. What Would Mystie Say ?

18. Where My Loved One Is Now

19. I Can Still Love

20A-B. I Can Help Myself

21. BREATHE

Activity 17
What Would Mystie Say?

Procedure:

- Show *For the Love of Emrys* to the children, asking them what they remember from the story.

- Ask children if they remember what Mystie said to Christina to help her feel better. Open the book to pg.20. Place the Mystie Mobile in front of the children and read what Mystie said to Christina.

- Ask children what they think Christina felt, after Mystie said her special words.

- Ask children what they think Mystie would say to them about their loved one dying.

Activity 18
Where My Loved One Is Now

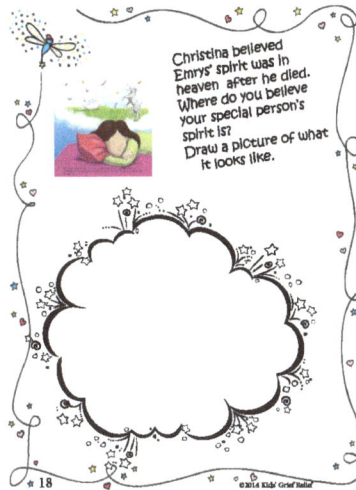

Christina believed Emrys' spirit was in heaven after he died. Where do you believe your special person's spirit is? Draw a picture of what it looks like.

18   ©2014 Kids' Grief Relief

Procedure:

- Read top of Activity 18 to children.

- After children draw a picture of where they believe their loved one is, ask them to share their drawing with the group.

Activity 19
I Can Still Love

Through her grief, Christina learned that the love in her heart is changeless. She will always love Emrys. She loved him when he was alive, and continues to love him even though he is gone.
Your love for your special person will be inside your heart forever, too.

Look at the heart below.
On the left side of the heart, write about how you showed love for your special person before he/she died.
On the right side write or draw pictures of how you show you still love him/her.

Procedure:

- Read top of Activity 19 to children.

- Ask children to describe the picture on the page. Remind children that the people in the picture are showing love for their person who has died.

- Read words next to the picture. It will probably be easier for children to come up with ways of showing love before the death of their loved one. Encourage children to think about ways they can still show love, even though their loved one has died.

- Some ideas might be visiting the gravesite, looking at pictures, talking about the happy times together, creating a special memorial place with things and pictures in their homes, creating a poem or song about the loved one, etc...

Activity 20
I Can Help Myself

Loving yourself by doing things you enjoy can help you move through grief. Think about ways you can help yourself to feel better. You can draw pictures or write down your ideas.

When I feel sad I Can

When I feel worried I Can

When I feel scared I Can

When I feel angry I Can

When I feel upset I Can

When I feel _____ I Can

What's your favorite thing to do? Close your eyes for a moment, and pretend you are doing it.

Now, _____ my wings to show how you feel when you're doing your favorite thing.

I know you can't fly like me, but you can feel like you're flying, when you're doing something you really enjoy.

Procedure:

- Read top of Activity 20 A.

- Next go over each box, and brainstorm ways for children to help themselves.

- As children come up with ideas to help themselves, remind them how brave they are to find ways to help them move through grief.

- Read Activity 20 B, inviting children to color in Mystie's wings. Ask children to share, when they are finished.

Activity 21
BREATHE

Here's another way to help yourself when you're feeling dragged—down.

It's all about BREATHING.

When you take the time to control how you breathe, you can help yourself handle some of the dragged—down emotions of grief. You will feel more relaxed and calm. Your body gets the air it needs to calm yourself down. That feels good.

breeathe

Procedure:

- Read Activity 21.

- Tell children you're going to show them how to do a bellybreath. Say, "**Belly breathing is one thing you can do when you feel grief. Belly breathing is about taking deep breaths. You breath so deep that you can feel it in your belly. Let's try together:**

  1. **First, put your hands on your belly.**
  2. **Now close your mouth and breath slowly through your nose.**
  3. **Count to 4 slowly, in your head, as you breath in.**
  4. **Hold the air in your body while you count to 4.**
  5. **Slowly let air out through your mouth or nose.**
  6. **Let's try again."   (repeat steps 1-5)**

- Say, "**What did you feel your belly do? When your belly goes up and down as you take deep breaths, you are belly breathing. How does that make you feel?**"

- Remind children to try this whenever they are feeling "dragged-down."

"... The bereaved child feels secure knowing that in the midst of any life-changing circumstance, there is something to rely on - Love! It is inside each of us all the time and can be accessed every moment of the day "...

from *The Evolution of Child Bereavement*
by Kids' Grief Relief

Session 5
My Thoughts Matter

Objectives

✦ Children discover thoughts that make them feel "dragged-down".

✦ Children practice ways to release negative thoughts.

✦ Children learn the power of thinking positive, loving thoughts.

✦ Children create positive affirmations about themselves.

Materials Needed:

Waste Basket
Scrap Paper
Hand Mirror

Session 5
My Thoughts Matter

Activities 22-26

Mystie's Activities

22. My Dragged-Down Thoughts

23. Throw Them Away !

24. Dragon-Fly Thoughts

25. Loving Thoughts

26. Frame Yourself !

Activity 22
My Dragged-Down Thoughts

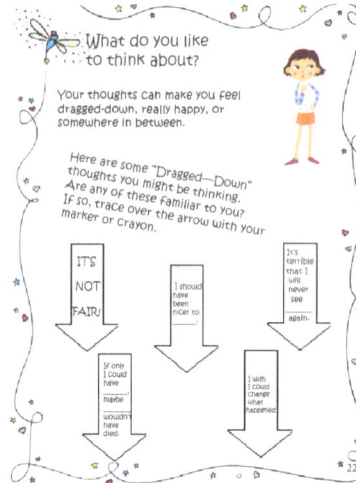

What do you like to think about?

Your thoughts can make you feel dragged-down, really happy, or somewhere in between.

Here are some "Dragged—Down" thoughts you might be thinking. Are any of these familiar to you? If so, trace over the arrow with your marker or crayon.

Procedure:

- Read question on top of Activity 22. Allow children time to answer.

- Read next two paragraphs.

- One at a time read the words in the arrows. Invite the children to walk around the room looking "dragged-down", if any particular phrase is some thought they have had since the death of their loved one.

- Ask each child to trace over the arrows that have the thoughts that dragged them down.

46

Activity 23
Throw Them Away!

Let's throw away all YOUR "Dragged—Down" thoughts.

Procedure:

- Read top of Activity 23.

- Tell children that it's time to throw all their "dragged-down" thoughts into the trash!

- Here are several ways to do this activity:

1. Tell children to think about a "dragged-down" thought. Direct them to pretend to pull it out of their head, and throw the thought into a trash can.

2. Children can write their "dragged-down" thoughts on a piece of paper, tear up the paper, and throw the scraps in the trashcan.

3. Children can write their dragged-down thoughts on paper, then glue them onto the picture of the trash can on Activity 23.

Activity 24
Dragon-Fly Thoughts!

Now it's time for dragon—fly thoughts! When you think a dragon—fly thought, you feel good inside. Then everything feels better.

Can you say these aloud?

1. I am brave.

2. I am smart enough to understand what happened.

3. It feels good to talk to others about what happened.

4. I have my own unique feelings about death.

5. I have special memories of _____ that I will always treasure.

6. I like who I am.

7. I am grateful for all the people who love me.

8. I am a powerful kid!

Procedure:

- Read top of Activity 24.

- Go over each statement, one at a time, giving each child a chance to say the words aloud.

- Using a hand-mirror ask children to say the statement, while looking at themselves in the mirror.

Activity 25
Loving Thoughts

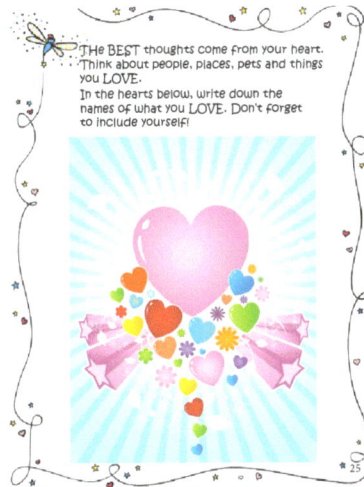

The BEST thoughts come from your heart. Think about people, places, pets and things you LOVE.
In the hearts below, write down the names of what you LOVE. Don't forget to include yourself!

Procedure:

- Read top of Activity 25.

- After children write the names of all the things they LOVE, ask them to share with the rest of the group.

Activity 26
Frame Yourself!

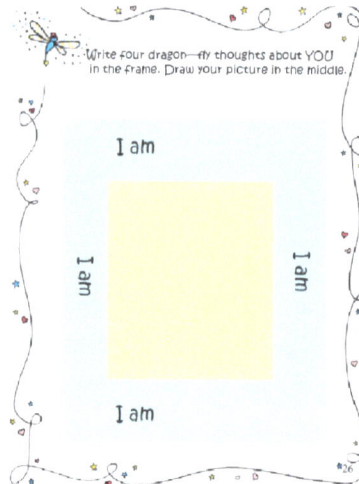

Write four dragon—fly thoughts about YOU in the frame. Draw your picture in the middle.

I am

I am   I am

I am

Procedure:

- Read top of Activity 26. Direct children to think of four positive statements about themselves. Encourage children to start each statement with "I am".

- Children write down their positive statements and draw a picture of themselves in the frame.

- Using a hand-mirror, invite each child to look in the mirror, then speak aloud the four affirmations listed on their frame.

- Tell children the next class is the final time they will meet as a group. Remind them to bring in a picture of their loved one. Tell them they will do a ceremony honoring their loved one, then have a celebration honoring their loved one and themselves, too!

"...As a child processes the difficult thoughts and emotions associated with grief, love all-ways triumphs. Our society is greatly blessed by compassionate children who grow up loving themselves and others"...

from *The Evolution of Child Bereavement*
by Kids' Grief Relief

Session 6
Ending Celebration

Objectives

- Children review what they have learned about grief.

- Children write a letter to their deceased loved one.

- Children share in a ceremony honoring their loved one.

- Children learn a rhyme to help them when they are "dragged-down".

- Children recognize themself as being a "powerful kid".

Materials Needed:

Battery operated tea-lights for each student
Scissors
Food and Drink for each student
Optional Graduation Gift for each student

(e.g. available from Kids' Grief Relief - see pg.4)

Session 6
Ending Celebration

Activities 27-31

Mystie's Activities

27. What I Know About Grief

28. Love Letter

29. Ceremony

30A-B. Words To Live By

31. I AM A Powerful Kid !

Activity 27
What I Know About Grief

You've done a great job learning
how to deal with the death of
your loved one. You are very brave!

Here are some statements about grief.
If you agree with the statement, draw one
heart next to it.
If you really, really agree with it, draw two
hearts next to it.
If you do not agree, draw an X next to it.

1. It's okay to cry when you feel sad.

2. It's normal to be upset and worried when someone you love has died.

3. Everyone grieves the same way.

4. I know it's okay to tell someone that I don't feel well because I am grieving.

5. I will miss _____ for a long time.

6. I can be happy again, even though _____ had died.

7. Hiding my feelings is a good way to feel better.

8. My positive thoughts help me feel better.

9. Acting out in school or at home is a good way to express grief.

10. Taking time to breath and relax helps me when I feel upset.

Procedure:

- Welcome children to their last session by congratulating them for coming to grief group and participating in the past sessions. Tell them they will be taking home their Activity Folder today.

- Ask children to look in their folders to see all they have accomplished and shared. Ask children how they feel about what they have done so far.

- Activity 27 is an assessment for the facilitator and the child. Read the top of the page, then do each sentence one by one, as directed.

Activity 28
Love Letter

Procedure:

- Tell children that part of the ceremony honoring their loved one is writing a letter to the deceased. Children will need some prompts to write the letter on Activity 28.

- You may want to write these on the wipe-off board or on a piece of paper to help them. If a child has difficulties in writing, the words should be dictated to someone who can write the letter for him/her.

- PROMPTS: I wanted to tell you...
            What I miss most about you is....
            I like to think about when we.....
            I will always remember....

Note:

Discuss the idea of putting their letter to their loved one in a special place. They may want to keep it in a decorated container or frame it for their room or home. Perhaps they want to bury it.

Activity 29
Ceremony Honoring Loved Ones

FOREVER CALENDAR

During each and every day,
We Love them.

During each and every night,
We Love them.

During each and every week,
We Love them.

During each and every month,
We Love them.

During each and every season,
We Love them.

During each and every year,
We Love them.

As the days turn into weeks, turn into months,
turn into seasons, turn into years,
We Love them;
Forever.

Procedure:

- Ask children if they understand what a calendar is. When you're satisfied with their understanding, tell them they're going to use a **Forever Calendar,** Activity 29.

- Ask, *"What do you think a **Forever Calendar** is?"* Then tell them it's a calendar that shows they will love their loved one forever.

- If you have the Mystie Mobile, place it on the table.

- Give each child a battery operated candle. Direct them to write the name of their loved one on the side of the plastic candle (sharpies work best).

- Create an empty space on a table, where children can place their candles in a circle. Children can place photos of their loved one next to their candle.

Activity 29
(Continued)

- One at a time, ask children to turn their candle on. Remind them that the light of the candle represents the love and light in their hearts, which will be present for their loved ones the rest of their lives.

- As the children light their candles, they may read their letters, one at a time.

- When all candles are lit, and each student has had the opportunity to read their letters, tell children it's time to read their **Forever Calendar**. If children cannot read the words of the Calendar, read it aloud and ask them to repeat the words.

- After the poem is read, ask children to turn their candle off, telling them to keep the candle as a special remembrance of their loved one.

- Tell children that in honor of their loved ones, and in honoring their committment to move through grief, there will be a celebration with food and drink.

- Hand out "Graduation Gift" (optional).

- ENJOY!

Note:
Kids' Grief Relief offers special mementos for students who have completed this course (e.g. Mystie Bracelet or Keychain).

Activity 30
Words To Live By

Bye Kids! I'm leaving you these powerful Heart—Words to say anytime you're feeling some grief.

The Power of my heart is strong
It gently guides me all day long.
If I feel sad throughout the day
This Love reminds me, I'm still okay!

Even though my life has changed
Since _____ has gone away,
There is one thing that's always there
It's Love inside my heart to share.

A-30

Procedure:

- As students end their celebration, invite them to read the top half of Activity 30.

- One at a time, ask students to read the words inside the frame.

Activity 31
I AM A Powerful Kid !

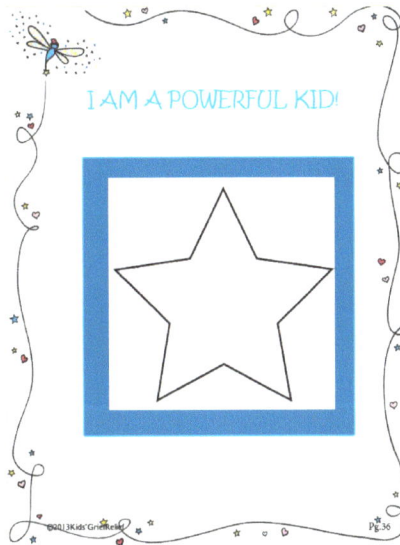

I AM A POWERFUL KID!

Procedure:

- Direct students to write their name in the star on Activity 31.

- As each student says, "I am a powerful kid!", all the other students reply, "You *are* a powerful kid!"

APPENDIX I
SPECIAL ACTIVITIES

(Downloadable from www.KidsGriefRelief.Org)

The following Activities can be used during any of the six sessions.

Some are specific to a time of year, others are special topics discussed in more depth than the session's activities.

They are all available for free !

Simply go to
www. KidsGriefRelief.org
and click on
"Downloads"

APPENDIX I
SPECIAL ACTIVITIES

Mystie tells tips on how
to feel like you're flying

Mystie's Magical
Message to Children

Remembering Someone
Special

Another Magical
Message from Mystie

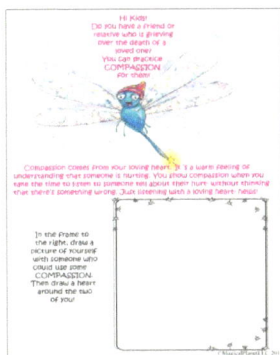

Mystie teaches
Practicing Compassion

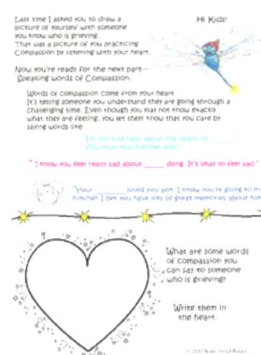

Mystie's Words of
Compassion

Mystie and Memory

Mystie's "I AM" Mirror

Mystie's Valentines Day Message

Mystie talks about Cremation

It's OK to have a "Dragged-Down" Day

Mystie asks, " What are you Thinking ? "

APPENDIX I
SPECIAL ACTIVITIES (continued)

Mystie says remember
to honor yourself

Mystie talsk about
Gratitude and Grief

Mystie talks about
back to school time

Mystie explains that
Sharing is Caring

Mystie talks about
Self-Worth

Mystie talks about
Giving Thanks

Mystie's Holiday
Special

Mystie talks about
starting a new year

Mystie talks about
putting your I AM first

Mystie talks about the
Greatest Strength of All

Mystie shows Parents
some Healing Themes

Mystie asks
"What's Changed ?"

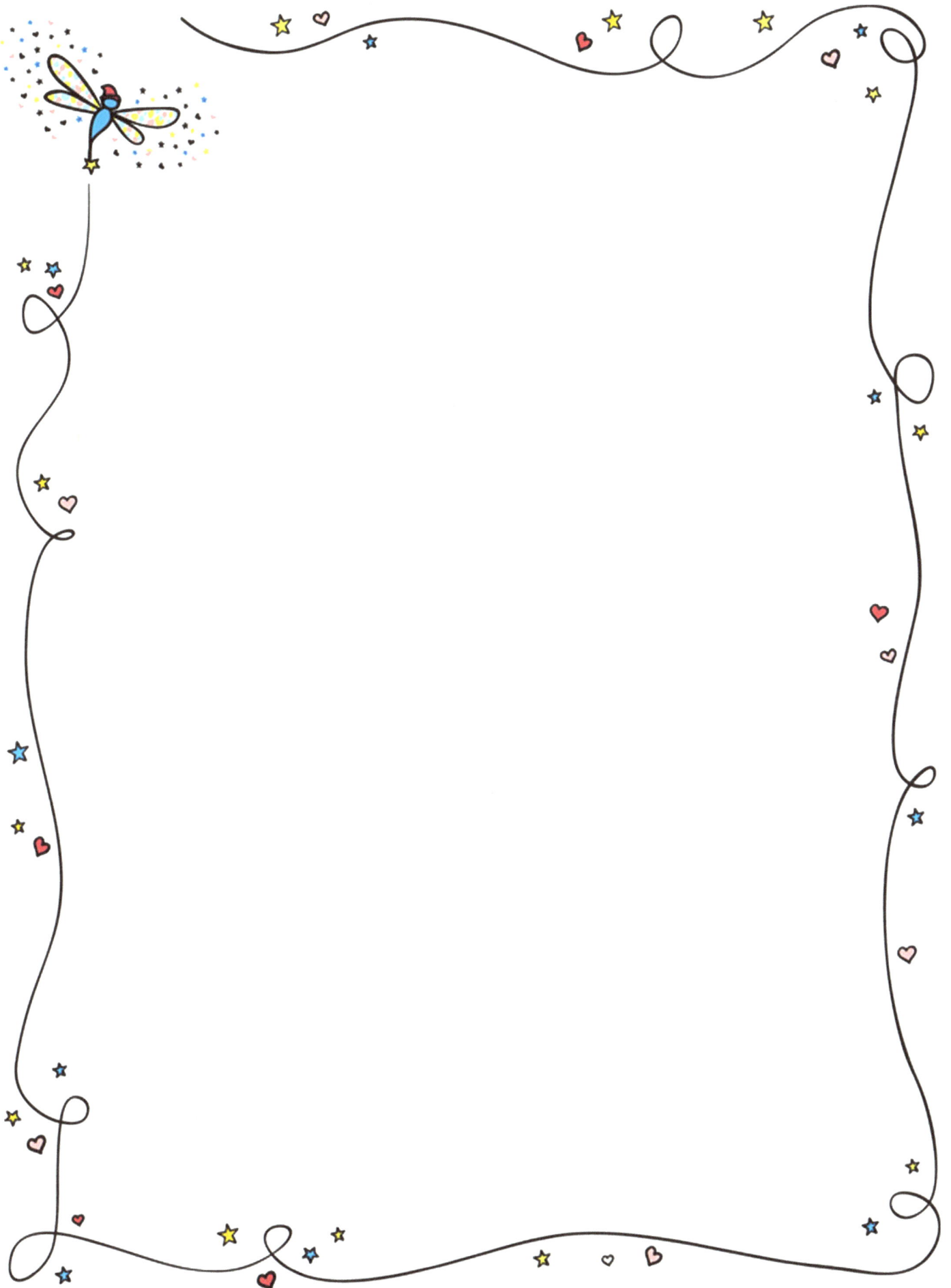

NOTES

www.ingramcontent.com/pod-product-compliance
Lightning Source LLC
LaVergne TN
LVHW072106070426
835509LV00002B/39